Inspiration

JOHN KEATS

Poetry

Publisher and Creative Director: Nick Wells
Commissioning Editor: Polly Prior
Art Director and Layout Design: Mike Spender
Digital Design and Production: Chris Herbert

FLAME TREE PUBLISHING
6 Melbray Mews
London SW6 3NS
United Kingdom
flametreepublishing.com

First published 2019

19 21 23 22 20
1 3 5 7 9 10 8 6 4 2

Every effort has been made to contact copyright holders. In the event of an oversight the publishers would be glad to rectify any omissions in future editions of this book.

A CIP record for this book is available from the British Library upon request.

ISBN 978-1-78755-276-0

Printed in China | Created, Developed & Produced in the United Kingdom

Inspiration

JOHN KEATS

Poetry

Introduction by
Ellen Nicholls

FLAME TREE
PUBLISHING

CONTENTS

INTRODUCTION

John Keats published only three collections of poetry before dying of consumption in Rome on 23 February 1821, at the age of 25. An avid reader and keenly attuned to the social and intellectual advances poets could make, Keats died not knowing if he had been successful in adding a meaningful poetic contribution to the 'grand march of intellect' (Letter to John Hamilton Reynolds, 3 May 1818). It was the richly sensual language, the subtle manipulation of poetic form and genre, and the beautifully complex engagement with uncertainties in the poetry of these three volumes (and the poetry that was unpublished at the time of his death), as well as his astonishingly insightful letters, that secured Keats's posthumous fame. Alongside poets such as Lord Byron and Percy Bysshe Shelley, Keats has become a key figure in British Romanticism and continues to hold a central place in the imagination of writers and readers alike.

Born in Moorgate, London, on 31 October 1795, Keats grew up in the lower-middle class environs of the city suburbs. After studying an unusually eclectic and forward-thinking curriculum at the dissenting school, Clarke's Academy in Enfield, London, Keats became an apprentice apothecary before continuing his medical training at the united hospitals of St Thomas and Guy's. Appointed as a surgeon's dresser at a time before effective surgical anaesthesia was introduced, Keats encountered scenes of extreme pain and sickness that would foster a profound interest in the responsibilities of the 'physician poet' as a figure who might pour 'a balm upon the world' (*The Fall of Hyperion*, Book I, 201). Fully integrated in Keats's imagination, poetry and medicine were the domains of the Greek God Apollo, a presence who recurs throughout Keats's poetry. This is most notable in the unfinished poem *Hyperion*, whose fallen Titans writhe around like patients upon an operating table, 'horribly convulsed/ With sanguine fev'rous boiling gurge of pulse' (*Hyperion*, Book II, 27–28). It was Keats's lower-middle class status as an apothecary-surgeon that would also come to inform a reviewer's scathing attack on his long and convoluted romance-epic *Endymion*. The reviewer denounced Keats's supposedly upstart, poetic ambitions; mocked his 'cockney rhymes'; and concluded: 'it is a better and a wiser thing to be a starved apothecary than a starved poet' (John Gibson Lockhart's Anonymous Review of *Endymion* in Blackwood's *Edinburgh* Magazine, 1818). Happily, Keats did not agree.

Though Keats left medicine to pursue a career in poetry, he remained invested in the life of bodily sensations, believing that 'axioms in

philosophy are not axioms until they are proved upon our pulses'
(Letter to John Hamilton Reynolds, 3 May 1818). After nursing his
brother Tom through terminal pulmonary tuberculosis – the disease
from which Keats himself would die – Keats extended his exploration
of the relationship between the pleasures of the imagination and the
'wakeful anguish' ('Ode on Melancholy', 10) of reality in poems such
as *The Eve of St Agnes*, *Isabella; Or, the Pot of Basil*, *Lamia*, and the
great odes of 1819. Keats called attention to the slipperiness between
ostensible dichotomies, dismantling the oppositions between
dreaming and reality, art and nature, pleasure and pain, feeling and
thinking. Proposing that the mind contained 'negative capability',
Keats firmly believed in the receptivity of the creative imagination
and the potential for the mind to exist in 'uncertainties, Mysteries,
doubts, without any irritable reaching after fact & reason' (Letter
to George and Tom Keats, December 1817). Complexities were
not 'knotty problem[s]' (*Lamia*, Part II, 160) to be deciphered and
unravelled, but enigmas to be embraced and explored.

Keats's poetic imagination survives, not as an overbearing or
egotistical presence that directs the reader towards incontrovertible
truths, but is positioned as a 'camelion' who 'has no self' (Letter
to Richard Woodhouse, 27 October 1818). Almost invisible, Keats
inhabits the subjects and intricacies he challenges his readers to

investigate, even as he undercuts any stable interpretation we might arrive at, thereby spotlighting the multiplicity and mutability of both the human condition and of truth itself.

What endures in the poems collected together in this edition is beautifully evocative language that indulges in its own sensory luxuriousness at the same time as it 'tease[s] us out of thought' ('Ode on a Grecian Urn', 44). This edition celebrates both the depth and breadth of Keats's 'teeming brain' ('When I Have Fears', 2) and his unique expression of the poetic imagination.

Ellen Nicholls

ON BEAUTY

A Thing of Beauty
is a Joy for Ever

To Solitude

O Solitude! if I must with thee dwell,
Let it not be among the jumbled heap
Of murky buildings; climb with me the steep,
Nature's observatory – whence the dell,
Its flowery slopes, its river's crystal swell,
May seem a span; let me thy vigils keep
'Mongst boughs pavillion'd, where the deer's swift leap
Startles the wild bee from the fox-glove bell.
But though I'll gladly trace these scenes with thee,
Yet the sweet converse of an innocent mind,
Whose words are images of thoughts refin'd,
Is my soul's pleasure; and it sure must be
Almost the highest bliss of human-kind,
When to thy haunts two kindred spirits flee.

1816

To One Who Has Been Long in City Pent

To one who has been long in city pent,
'Tis very sweet to look into the fair
And open face of heaven, – to breathe a prayer
Full in the smile of the blue firmament.
Who is more happy, when, with heart's content,
Fatigued he sinks into some pleasant lair
Of wavy grass, and reads a debonair
And gentle tale of love and languishment?
Returning home at evening, with an ear
Catching the notes of Philomel, – an eye
Watching the sailing cloudlet's bright career,
He mourns that day so soon has glided by:
E'en like the passage of an angel's tear
That falls through the clear ether silently.

1816

SUMMER'S EVE

Oh! how I love, on a fair summer's eve,
When streams of light pour down the golden west,
And on the balmy zephyrs tranquil rest
The silver clouds, far – far away to leave
All meaner thoughts, and take a sweet reprieve
From little cares; to find, with easy quest,
A fragrant wild, with Nature's beauty drest,
And there into delight my soul deceive.
There warm my breast with patriotic lore,
Musing on Milton's fate – on Sydney's bier –
Till their stern forms before my mind arise:
Perhaps on wing of Poesy upsoar,
Full often dropping a delicious tear,
When some melodious sorrow spells mine eyes.

1816

To a Friend Who Sent Me Some Roses

As late I rambled in the happy fields,
What time the skylark shakes the tremulous dew
From his lush clover covert; – when anew
Adventurous knights take up their dinted shields;
I saw the sweetest flower wild nature yields,
A fresh-blown musk-rose; 'twas the first that threw
Its sweets upon the summer: graceful it grew
As is the wand that Queen Titania wields.
And, as I feasted on its fragrancy,
I thought the garden-rose it far excell'd;
But when, O Wells! thy roses came to me,
My sense with their deliciousness was spell'd:
Soft voices had they, that with tender plea
Whispered of peace, and truth, and friendliness unquell'd.

1816

HOW MANY BARDS

How many bards gild the lapses of time!
A few of them have ever been the food
Of my delighted fancy, – I could brood
Over their beauties, earthly, or sublime:
And often, when I sit me down to rhyme,
These will in throngs before my mind intrude:
But no confusion, no disturbance rude
Do they occasion; 'tis a pleasing chime.
So the unnumber'd sounds that evening store;
The songs of birds – the whisp'ring of the leaves –
The voice of waters – the great bell that heaves
With solemn sound, – and thousand others more,
That distance of recognizance bereaves,
Make pleasing music, and not wild uproar.

1816

I Stood Tip-Toe Upon a Little Hill (Extract)

I stood tip-toe upon a little hill,
The air was cooling, and so very still,
That the sweet buds which with a modest pride
Pull droopingly, in slanting curve aside,
Their scantly leaved, and finely tapering stems,
Had not yet lost those starry diadems
Caught from the early sobbing of the morn.
The clouds were pure and white as flocks new shorn,
And fresh from the clear brook; sweetly they slept
On the blue fields of heaven, and then there crept
A little noiseless noise among the leaves,
Born of the very sigh that silence heaves:
For not the faintest motion could be seen
Of all the shades that slanted o'er the green.
There was wide wand'ring for the greediest eye,
To peer about upon variety;
Far round the horizon's crystal air to skim,
And trace the dwindled edgings of its brim;
To picture out the quaint, and curious bending
Of a fresh woodland alley, never ending;
Or by the bowery clefts, and leafy shelves,

Guess where the jaunty streams refresh themselves.
I gazed awhile, and felt as light, and free
As though the fanning wings of Mercury
Had played upon my heels: I was light-hearted,
And many pleasures to my vision started;
So I straightway began to pluck a posey
Of luxuries bright, milky, soft and rosy.

A bush of May flowers with the bees about them;
Ah, sure no tasteful nook would be without them;
And let a lush laburnum oversweep them,
And let long grass grow round the roots to keep them
Moist, cool and green; and shade the violets,
That they may bind the moss in leafy nets.

A filbert hedge with wildbriar overtwined,
And clumps of woodbine taking the soft wind
Upon their summer thrones; there too should be
The frequent chequer of a youngling tree,
That with a score of light green brethren shoots
From the quaint mossiness of aged roots:
Round which is heard a spring-head of clear waters
Babbling so wildly of its lovely daughters

The spreading blue bells: it may haply mourn

That such fair clusters should be rudely torn

From their fresh beds, and scatter'd thoughtlessly

By infant hands, left on the path to die.

Open afresh your round of starry folds,

Ye ardent marigolds!

Dry up the moisture from your golden lids,

For great Apollo bids

That in these days your praises should be sung

On many harps, which he has lately strung;

And when again your dewiness he kisses,

Tell him, I have you in my world of blisses:

So haply when I rove in some far vale,

His mighty voice may come upon the gale.

1816

On the Grasshopper and Cricket

The poetry of earth is never dead:
When all the birds are faint with the hot sun,
And hide in cooling trees, a voice will run
From hedge to hedge about the new-mown mead;
That is the Grasshopper's – he takes the lead
In summer luxury, – he has never done
With his delights; for when tired out with fun
He rests at ease beneath some pleasant weed.
The poetry of earth is ceasing never:
On a lone winter evening, when the frost
Has wrought a silence, from the stove there shrills
The Cricket's song, in warmth increasing ever,
And seems to one in drowsiness half lost,
The Grasshopper's among some grassy hills.

1816

To G.A.W.

Nymph of the downward smile, and sidelong glance,
In what diviner moments of the day
Art thou most lovely? when gone far astray
Into the labyrinths of sweet utterance?
Or when serenely wandering in a trance
Of sober thought? Or when starting away,
With careless robe, to meet the morning ray,
Thou sparest the flowers in thy mazy dance?
Haply 'tis when thy ruby lips part sweetly,
And so remain, because thou listenest:
But thou to please wert nurtured so completely
That I can never tell what mood is best.
I shall as soon pronounce which grace more neatly
Trips it before Apollo than the rest.

1817

ON LEIGH HUNT'S POEM, THE 'STORY OF RIMINI'

Who loves to peer up at the morning sun,
With half-shut eyes and comfortable cheek,
Let him, with this sweet tale, full often seek
For meadows where the little rivers run;
Who loves to linger with that brightest one
Of Heaven – Hesperus – let him lowly speak
These numbers to the night, and starlight meek,
Or moon, if that her hunting be begun.
He who knows these delights, and too is prone
To moralize upon a smile or tear,
Will find at once a region of his own,
A bower for his spirit, and will steer
To alleys where the fir-tree drops its cone,
Where robins hop, and fallen leaves are sear.

1817

ON THE SEA

It keeps eternal whisperings around
Desolate shores, and with its mighty swell
Gluts twice ten thousand caverns, till the spell
Of Hecate leaves them their old shadowy sound.
Often 'tis in such gentle temper found,
That scarcely will the very smallest shell
Be moved for days from where it sometime fell.
When last the winds of Heaven were unbound.
Oh, ye! who have your eyeballs vexed and tired,
Feast them upon the wideness of the Sea;
Oh ye! whose ears are dinned with uproar rude,
Or fed too much with cloying melody, –
Sit ye near some old cavern's mouth and brood,
Until ye start, as if the sea nymphs quired!

1817

ENDYMION (EXTRACT, BOOK I)

A thing of beauty is a joy for ever:
Its loveliness increases; it will never
Pass into nothingness; but still will keep
A bower quiet for us, and a sleep
Full of sweet dreams, and health, and quiet breathing.
Therefore, on every morrow, are we wreathing
A flowery band to bind us to the earth,
Spite of despondence, of the inhuman dearth
Of noble natures, of the gloomy days,
Of all the unhealthy and o'er-darkened ways
Made for our searching: yes, in spite of all,
Some shape of beauty moves away the pall
From our dark spirits. Such the sun, the moon,
Trees old and young, sprouting a shady boon
For simple sheep; and such are daffodils
With the green world they live in; and clear rills
That for themselves a cooling covert make
'Gainst the hot season; the mid forest brake,
Rich with a sprinkling of fair musk-rose blooms:
And such too is the grandeur of the dooms
We have imagined for the mighty dead;

All lovely tales that we have heard or read:
An endless fountain of immortal drink,
Pouring unto us from the heaven's brink.

Nor do we merely feel these essences
For one short hour; no, even as the trees
That whisper round a temple become soon
Dear as the temple's self, so does the moon,
The passion poesy, glories infinite,
Haunt us till they become a cheering light
Unto our souls, and bound to us so fast,
That, whether there be shine, or gloom o'ercast,
They alway must be with us, or we die.

Therefore, 'tis with full happiness that I
Will trace the story of Endymion.
The very music of the name has gone
Into my being, and each pleasant scene
Is growing fresh before me as the green
Of our own vallies: so I will begin
Now while I cannot hear the city's din;
Now while the early budders are just new,
And run in mazes of the youngest hue

About old forests; while the willow trails
Its delicate amber; and the dairy pails
Bring home increase of milk. And, as the year
Grows lush in juicy stalks, I'll smoothly steer
My little boat, for many quiet hours,
With streams that deepen freshly into bowers.
Many and many a verse I hope to write,
Before the daisies, vermeil rimm'd and white,
Hide in deep herbage; and ere yet the bees
Hum about globes of clover and sweet peas,
I must be near the middle of my story.
O may no wintry season, bare and hoary,
See it half finished: but let Autumn bold,
With universal tinge of sober gold,
Be all about me when I make an end.
And now at once, adventuresome, I send
My herald thought into a wilderness:
There let its trumpet blow, and quickly dress
My uncertain path with green, that I may speed
Easily onward, thorough flowers and weed.

1817–18

Endymion (Extract, Book I, 'Hymn to Pan')

'O thou, whose mighty palace roof doth hang
From jagged trunks, and overshadoweth
Eternal whispers, glooms, the birth, life, death
Of unseen flowers in heavy peacefulness;
Who lovest to see the hamadryads dress
Their ruffled locks where meeting hazels darken;
And through whole solemn hours dost sit, and hearken
The dreary melody of bedded reeds –
In desolate places, where dank moisture breeds
The pipy hemlock to strange overgrowth;
Bethinking thee, how melancholy loth
Thou wast to lose fair Syrinx – do thou now,
By thy love's milky brow!
By all the trembling mazes that she ran,
Hear us, great Pan!

'O thou, for whose soul-soothing quiet, turtles
Passion their voices cooingly 'mong myrtles,
What time thou wanderest at eventide
Through sunny meadows, that outskirt the side
Of thine enmossed realms: O thou, to whom

Broad leaved fig trees even now foredoom

Their ripen'd fruitage; yellow girted bees

Their golden honeycombs; our village leas

Their fairest-blossom'd beans and poppied corn;

The chuckling linnet its five young unborn,

To sing for thee; low creeping strawberries

Their summer coolness; pent up butterflies

Their freckled wings; yea, the fresh budding year

All its completions – be quickly near,

By every wind that nods the mountain pine,

O forester divine!

'Thou, to whom every fawn and satyr flies

For willing service; whether to surprise

The squatted hare while in half sleeping fit;

Or upward ragged precipices flit

To save poor lambkins from the eagle's maw;

Or by mysterious enticement draw

Bewildered shepherds to their path again;

Or to tread breathless round the frothy main,

And gather up all fancifullest shells

For thee to tumble into Naiads' cells,

And, being hidden, laugh at their out-peeping;

Or to delight thee with fantastic leaping,
The while they pelt each other on the crown
With silvery oak apples, and fir cones brown –
By all the echoes that about thee ring,
Hear us, O satyr king!

'O Hearkener to the loud clapping shears,
While ever and anon to his shorn peers
A ram goes bleating: Winder of the horn,
When snouted wild-boars routing tender corn
Anger our huntsman: Breather round our farms,
To keep off mildews, and all weather harms:
Strange ministrant of undescribed sounds,
That come a swooning over hollow grounds,
And wither drearily on barren moors:
Dread opener of the mysterious doors
Leading to universal knowledge – see,
Great son of Dryope,
The many that are come to pay their vows
With leaves about their brows!

'Be still the unimaginable lodge
For solitary thinkings; such as dodge

Conception to the very bourne of heaven,

Then leave the naked brain: be still the leaven,

That spreading in this dull and clodded earth

Gives it a touch ethereal – a new birth:

Be still a symbol of immensity;

A firmament reflected in a sea;

An element filling the space between;

An unknown – but no more: we humbly screen

With uplift hands our foreheads, lowly bending,

And giving out a shout most heaven rending,

Conjure thee to receive our humble Paean,

Upon thy Mount Lycean!'

1818

DAISY'S SONG

The sun, with his great eye,
Sees not so much as I;
And the moon, all silver-proud,
Might as well be in a cloud.

And O the spring – the spring
I lead the life of a king!
Couch'd in the teeming grass,
I spy each pretty lass.

I look where no one dares,
And I stare where no one stares,
And when the night is nigh,
Lambs bleat my lullaby.

1818

Answer to a Sonnet by J.H. Reynolds, Ending

'Dark eyes are dearer far
Than those that mock the hyacinthine bell.'

Blue! 'Tis the life of heaven, – the domain
Of Cynthia, – the wide palace of the sun, –
The tent of Hesperus, and all his train, –
The bosomer of clouds, gold, gray, and dun.
Blue! 'Tis the life of waters: – Ocean
And all its vassal streams, pools numberless,
May rage, and foam, and fret, but never can
Subside, if not to dark-blue nativeness.
Blue! gentle cousin of the forest-green,
Married to green in all the sweetest flowers –
Forget-me-not, – the blue-bell, – and, that queen
Of secrecy, the violet: what strange powers
Hast thou, as a mere shadow! But how great,
When in an Eye thou art alive with fate!

1818

Meg Merrilies

Old Meg she was a Gipsy,
And liv'd upon the Moors:
Her bed it was the brown heath turf,
And her house was out of doors.

Her apples were swart blackberries,
Her currants pods o' broom;
Her wine was dew of the wild white rose,
Her book a churchyard tomb.

Her Brothers were the craggy hills,
Her Sisters larchen trees –
Alone with her great family
She liv'd as she did please.

No breakfast had she many a morn,
No dinner many a noon,
And 'stead of supper she would stare
Full hard against the Moon.

But every morn of woodbine fresh
She made her garlanding,
And every night the dark glen Yew
She wove, and she would sing.

And with her fingers old and brown
She plaited Mats o' Rushes,
And gave them to the Cottagers
She met among the Bushes.

Old Meg was brave as Margaret Queen
And tall as Amazon:
An old red blanket cloak she wore;
A chip hat had she on.
God rest her aged bones somewhere –
She died full long agone!

1818

TO AILSA ROCK

Hearken, thou craggy ocean pyramid!
Give answer from thy voice – the sea-fowl's screams!
When were thy shoulders mantled in huge streams?
Whenfrom the sun was thy broad forehead hid?
How long is't since the mighty Power bid
Thee heave to airy sleep from fathom dreams –
Sleep in the lap of thunder or sunbeams –
Or when gray clouds are thy cold coverlid?
Thou answerest not, for thou art dead asleep.
Thy life is but two dead eternities,
The last in air, the former in the deep!
First with the whales, last with the eagle skies!
Drown'd wast thou till an earthquake made thee steep,
Another cannot wake thy giant size!

1818

Written Upon the Top of Ben Nevis

Read me a lesson, Muse, and speak it loud
Upon the top of Nevis, blind in mist!
I look into the chasms, and a shroud
Vapourous doth hide them, – just so much I wist
Mankind do know of hell; I look o'erhead,
And there is sullen mist, – even so much
Mankind can tell of heaven; mist is spread
Before the earth, beneath me, – even such,
Even so vague is man's sight of himself!
Here are the craggy stones beneath my feet, –
Thus much I know that, a poor witless elf,
I tread on them, – that all my eye doth meet
Is mist and crag, not only on this height,
But in the world of thought and mental might!

1818

WELCOME JOY, AND WELCOME SORROW

'Under the flag
Of each his faction, they to battle bring
Their embryon atoms.' – Milton

Welcome joy, and welcome sorrow,
Lethe's weed and Hermes' feather;
Come to-day, and come to-morrow,
I do love you both together!
I love to mark sad faces in fair weather;
And hear a merry laugh amid the thunder;
Fair and foul I love together.
Meadows sweet where flames are under,
And a giggle at a wonder;
Visage sage at pantomime;
Funeral, and steeple-chime;
Infant playing with a skull;
Morning fair, and shipwreck'd hull;
Nightshade with the woodbine kissing;
Serpents in red roses hissing;
Cleopatra regal-dress'd
With the aspic at her breast;

Dancing music, music sad,
Both together, sane and mad;
Muses bright and muses pale;
Sombre Saturn, Momus hale; –
Laugh and sigh, and laugh again;
Oh the sweetness of the pain!
Muses bright, and muses pale,
Bare your faces of the veil;
Let me see; and let me write
Of the day, and of the night –
Both together: – let me slake
All my thirst for sweet heart-ache!
Let my bower be of yew,
Interwreath'd with myrtles new;
Pines and lime-trees full in bloom,
And my couch a low grass-tomb.

1818

Ode on a Grecian Urn

Thou still unravish'd bride of quietness,
Thou foster-child of silence and slow time,
Sylvan historian, who canst thus express
A flowery tale more sweetly than our rhyme:
What leaf-fring'd legend haunts about thy shape
Of deities or mortals, or of both,
In Tempe or the dales of Arcady?
What men or gods are these? What maidens loth?
What mad pursuit? What struggle to escape?
What pipes and timbrels? What wild ecstasy?

Heard melodies are sweet, but those unheard
Are sweeter; therefore, ye soft pipes, play on;
Not to the sensual ear, but, more endear'd,
Pipe to the spirit ditties of no tone:
Fair youth, beneath the trees, thou canst not leave
Thy song, nor ever can those trees be bare;
Bold Lover, never, never canst thou kiss,
Though winning near the goal yet, do not grieve;
She cannot fade, though thou hast not thy bliss,
For ever wilt thou love, and she be fair!

Ah, happy, happy boughs! that cannot shed
Your leaves, nor ever bid the Spring adieu;
And, happy melodist, unwearied,
For ever piping songs for ever new;
More happy love! more happy, happy love!
For ever warm and still to be enjoy'd,
For ever panting, and for ever young;
All breathing human passion far above,
That leaves a heart high-sorrowful and cloy'd,
A burning forehead, and a parching tongue.

Who are these coming to the sacrifice?
To what green altar, O mysterious priest,
Lead'st thou that heifer lowing at the skies,
And all her silken flanks with garlands drest?
What little town by river or sea shore,
Or mountain-built with peaceful citadel,
Is emptied of this folk, this pious morn?
And, little town, thy streets for evermore
Will silent be; and not a soul to tell
Why thou art desolate, can e'er return.

O Attic shape! Fair attitude! with brede
Of marble men and maidens overwrought,
With forest branches and the trodden weed;
Thou, silent form, dost tease us out of thought
As doth eternity: Cold Pastoral!
When old age shall this generation waste,
Thou shalt remain, in midst of other woe
Than ours, a friend to man, to whom thou say'st,
'Beauty is truth, truth beauty, – that is all
Ye know on earth, and all ye need to know.'

1819

To Autumn

Season of mists and mellow fruitfulness,
Close bosom-friend of the maturing sun;
Conspiring with him how to load and bless
With fruit the vines that round the thatch-eves run;
To bend with apples the moss'd cottage-trees,
And fill all fruit with ripeness to the core;
To swell the gourd, and plump the hazel shells
With a sweet kernel; to set budding more,
And still more, later flowers for the bees,
Until they think warm days will never cease,
For summer has o'er-brimm'd their clammy cells.

Who hath not seen thee oft amid thy store?
Sometimes whoever seeks abroad may find
Thee sitting careless on a granary floor,
Thy hair soft-lifted by the winnowing wind;
Or on a half-reap'd furrow sound asleep,
Drows'd with the fume of poppies, while thy hook
Spares the next swath and all its twined flowers:
And sometimes like a gleaner thou dost keep
Steady thy laden head across a brook;

Or by a cyder-press, with patient look,
Thou watchest the last oozings hours by hours.

Where are the songs of spring? Ay, Where are they?
Think not of them, thou hast thy music too, –
While barred clouds bloom the soft-dying day,
And touch the stubble-plains with rosy hue;
Then in a wailful choir the small gnats mourn
Among the river sallows, borne aloft
Or sinking as the light wind lives or dies;
And full-grown lambs loud bleat from hilly bourn;
Hedge-crickets sing; and now with treble soft
The red-breast whistles from a garden-croft;
And gathering swallows twitter in the skies.

1819

BRIGHT STAR

Bright star! would I were stedfast as thou art –
Not in lone splendour hung aloft the night
And watching, with eternal lids apart,
Like nature's patient, sleepless Eremite,
The moving waters at their priestlike task
Of pure ablution round earth's human shores,
Or gazing on the new soft-fallen mask
Of snow upon the mountains and the moors –
No – yet still stedfast, still unchangeable,
Pillow'd upon my fair love's ripening breast,
To feel for ever its soft fall and swell,
Awake for ever in a sweet unrest,
Still, still to hear her tender-taken breath,
And so live ever – or else swoon to death.

1819

ON DREAMS

Do I Wake or Sleep?

ON PEACE

O Peace! and dost thou with thy presence bless
The dwellings of this war-surrounded Isle;
Soothing with placid brow our late distress,
Making the triple kingdom brightly smile?
Joyful I hail thy presence; and I hail
The sweet companions that await on thee;
Complete my joy let not my first wish fail,
Let the sweet mountain nymph thy favourite be,
With England's happiness proclaim Europa's Liberty.
O Europe! let not sceptred tyrants see
That thou must shelter in thy former state;
Keep thy chains burst, and boldly say thou art free;
Give thy kings law leave not uncurbed the great;
So with the horrors past thou'lt win thy happier fate!

1814

ON LEAVING SOME FRIENDS AT AN EARLY HOUR

Give me a golden pen, and let me lean
On heap'd up flowers, in regions clear, and far;
Bring me a tablet whiter than a star,
Or hand of hymning angel, when 'tis seen
The silver strings of heavenly harp atween:
And let there glide by many a pearly car,
Pink robes, and wavy hair, and diamond jar,
And half-discover'd wings, and glances keen.
The while let music wander round my ears,
And as it reaches each delicious ending,
Let me write down a line of glorious tone,
And full of many wonders of the spheres:
For what a height my spirit is contending!
'Tis not content so soon to be alone.

1816

Keen, Fitful Gusts

Keen, fitful gusts are whisp'ring here and there
Among the bushes half leafless, and dry;
The stars look very cold about the sky,
And I have many miles on foot to fare.
Yet feel I little of the cool bleak air,
Or of the dead leaves rustling drearily,
Or of those silver lamps that burn on high,
Or of the distance from home's pleasant lair:
For I am brimfull of the friendliness
That in a little cottage I have found;
Of fair-hair'd Milton's eloquent distress,
And all his love for gentle Lycid drown'd;
Of lovely Laura in her light green dress,
And faithful Petrarch gloriously crown'd.

1816

HAPPY IS ENGLAND! I COULD BE CONTENT

Happy is England! I could be content
To see no other verdure than its own;
To feel no other breezes than are blown
Through its tall woods with high romances blent:
Yet do I sometimes feel a languishment
For skies Italian, and an inward groan
To sit upon an Alp as on a throne,
And half forget what world or worldling meant.
Happy is England, sweet her artless daughters;
Enough their simple loveliness for me,
Enough their whitest arms in silence clinging:
Yet do I often warmly burn to see
Beauties of deeper glance, and hear their singing,
And float with them about the summer waters.

1816

On Seeing the Elgin Marbles

My spirit is too weak – mortality
Weighs heavily on me like unwilling sleep,
And each imagined pinnacle and steep
Of godlike hardship tells me I must die
Like a sick eagle looking at the sky.
Yet 'tis a gentle luxury to weep
That I have not the cloudy winds to keep
Fresh for the opening of the morning's eye.
Such dim-conceived glories of the brain
Bring round the heart an undescribable feud;
So do these wonders a most dizzy pain,
That mingles Grecian grandeur with the rude
Wasting of old time – with a billowy main –
A sun – a shadow of a magnitude.

1817

On Sitting Down to Read King Lear Once Again

O golden-tongued Romance with serene lute!
Fair plumed Syren! Queen of far away!
Leave melodizing on this wintry day,
Shut up thine olden pages, and be mute:
Adieu! for once again the fierce dispute,
Betwixt damnation and impassion'd clay
Must I burn through; once more humbly assay
The bitter-sweet of this Shakespearian fruit.
Chief Poet! and ye clouds of Albion,
Begetters of our deep eternal theme,
When through the old oak forest I am gone,
Let me not wander in a barren dream,
But when I am consumed in the fire,
Give me new Phoenix wings to fly at my desire.

1818

On Visiting the Tomb of Burns

The town, the churchyard, and the setting sun,
The clouds, the trees, the rounded hills all seem,
Though beautiful, cold – strange – as in a dream
I dreamed long ago, now new begun.
The short-liv'd, paly summer is but won
From winter's ague for one hour's gleam;
Through sapphire warm their stars do never beam:
All is cold Beauty; pain is never done.
For who has mind to relish, Minos-wise,
The real of Beauty, free from that dead hue
Sickly imagination and sick pride
Cast wan upon it? Burns! with honour due
I oft have honour'd thee. Great shadow, hide
Thy face; I sin against thy native skies.

1818

Fancy

Ever let the Fancy roam,
Pleasure never is at home:
At a touch sweet Pleasure melteth,
Like to bubbles when rain pelteth;
Then let winged Fancy wander
Through the thought still spread beyond her:
Open wide the mind's cage-door,
She'll dart forth, and cloudward soar.
O sweet Fancy! let her loose;
Summer's joys are spoilt by use,
And the enjoying of the Spring
Fades as does its blossoming;
Autumn's red-lipp'd fruitage too,
Blushing through the mist and dew,
Cloys with tasting: What do then?
Sit thee by the ingle, when
The sear faggot blazes bright,
Spirit of a winter's night;
When the soundless earth is muffled,
And the caked snow is shuffled
From the ploughboy's heavy shoon;

When the Night doth meet the Noon

In a dark conspiracy

To banish Even from her sky.

Sit thee there, and send abroad,

With a mind self-overaw'd,

Fancy, high-commission'd: – send her!

She has vassals to attend her:

She will bring, in spite of frost,

Beauties that the earth hath lost;

She will bring thee, all together,

All delights of summer weather;

All the buds and bells of May,

From dewy sward or thorny spray;

All the heaped Autumn's wealth,

With a still, mysterious stealth:

She will mix these pleasures up

Like three fit wines in a cup,

And thou shalt quaff it: – thou shalt hear

Distant harvest-carols clear;

Rustle of the reaped corn;

Sweet birds antheming the morn:

And, in the same moment, hark!

'Tis the early April lark,

Or the rooks, with busy caw,
Foraging for sticks and straw.
Thou shalt, at one glance, behold
The daisy and the marigold;
White-plum'd lillies, and the first
Hedge-grown primrose that hath burst;
Shaded hyacinth, alway
Sapphire queen of the mid-May;
And every leaf, and every flower
Pearled with the self-same shower.
Thou shalt see the field-mouse peep
Meagre from its celled sleep;
And the snake all winter-thin
Cast on sunny bank its skin;
Freckled nest-eggs thou shalt see
Hatching in the hawthorn-tree,
When the hen-bird's wing doth rest
Quiet on her mossy nest;
Then the hurry and alarm
When the bee-hive casts its swarm;
Acorns ripe down-pattering,
While the autumn breezes sing.

Oh, sweet Fancy! let her loose;
Every thing is spoilt by use:
Where's the cheek that doth not fade,
Too much gaz'd at? Where's the maid
Whose lip mature is ever new?
Where's the eye, however blue,
Doth not weary? Where's the face
One would meet in every place?
Where's the voice, however soft,
One would hear so very oft?
At a touch sweet Pleasure melteth
Like to bubbles when rain pelteth.
Let, then, winged Fancy find
Thee a mistress to thy mind:
Dulcet-ey'd as Ceres' daughter,
Ere the God of Torment taught her
How to frown and how to chide;
With a waist and with a side
White as Hebe's, when her zone
Slipt its golden clasp, and down
Fell her kirtle to her feet,
While she held the goblet sweet
And Jove grew languid. – Break the mesh

Of the Fancy's silken leash;
Quickly break her prison-string
And such joys as these she'll bring. –
Let the winged Fancy roam,
Pleasure never is at home.

1818

THE EVE OF ST AGNES

St. Agnes' Eve – Ah, bitter chill it was!
The owl, for all his feathers, was a-cold;
The hare limp'd trembling through the frozen grass,
And silent was the flock in woolly fold:
Numb were the Beadsman's fingers, while he told
His rosary, and while his frosted breath,
Like pious incense from a censer old,
Seem'd taking flight for heaven, without a death,
Past the sweet Virgin's picture, while his prayer he saith.

His prayer he saith, this patient, holy man;
Then takes his lamp, and riseth from his knees,
And back returneth, meagre, barefoot, wan,
Along the chapel aisle by slow degrees:
The sculptur'd dead, on each side, seem to freeze,
Emprison'd in black, purgatorial rails:
Knights, ladies, praying in dumb orat'ries,
He passeth by; and his weak spirit fails
To think how they may ache in icy hoods and mails.

Northward he turneth through a little door,
And scarce three steps, ere Music's golden tongue
Flatter'd to tears this aged man and poor;
But no – already had his deathbell rung;
The joys of all his life were said and sung:
His was harsh penance on St. Agnes' Eve:
Another way he went, and soon among
Rough ashes sat he for his soul's reprieve,
And all night kept awake, for sinners' sake to grieve.

That ancient Beadsman heard the prelude soft;
And so it chanc'd, for many a door was wide,
From hurry to and fro. Soon, up aloft,
The silver, snarling trumpets 'gan to chide:
The level chambers, ready with their pride,
Were glowing to receive a thousand guests:
The carved angels, ever eager-eyed,
Star'd, where upon their heads the cornice rests,
With hair blown back, and wings put cross-wise on
    their breasts.

At length burst in the argent revelry,

With plume, tiara, and all rich array,

Numerous as shadows haunting faerily

The brain, new stuff'd, in youth, with triumphs gay

Of old romance. These let us wish away,

And turn, sole-thoughted, to one Lady there,

Whose heart had brooded, all that wintry day,

On love, and wing'd St. Agnes' saintly care,

As she had heard old dames full many times declare.

They told her how, upon St. Agnes' Eve,

Young virgins might have visions of delight,

And soft adorings from their loves receive

Upon the honey'd middle of the night,

If ceremonies due they did aright;

As, supperless to bed they must retire,

And couch supine their beauties, lily white;

Nor look behind, nor sideways, but require

Of Heaven with upward eyes for all that they desire.

Full of this whim was thoughtful Madeline:
The music, yearning like a God in pain,
She scarcely heard: her maiden eyes divine,
Fix'd on the floor, saw many a sweeping train
Pass by – she heeded not at all: in vain
Came many a tiptoe, amorous cavalier,
And back retir'd; not cool'd by high disdain,
But she saw not: her heart was otherwhere:
She sigh'd for Agnes' dreams, the sweetest of the year.

She danc'd along with vague, regardless eyes,
Anxious her lips, her breathing quick and short:
The hallow'd hour was near at hand: she sighs
Amid the timbrels, and the throng'd resort
Of whisperers in anger, or in sport;
'Mid looks of love, defiance, hate, and scorn,
Hoodwink'd with faery fancy; all amort,
Save to St. Agnes and her lambs unshorn,
And all the bliss to be before to-morrow morn.

So, purposing each moment to retire,
She linger'd still. Meantime, across the moors,
Had come young Porphyro, with heart on fire
For Madeline. Beside the portal doors,
Buttress'd from moonlight, stands he, and implores
All saints to give him sight of Madeline,
But for one moment in the tedious hours,
That he might gaze and worship all unseen;
Perchance speak, kneel, touch, kiss – in sooth such things
        have been.

He ventures in: let no buzz'd whisper tell:
All eyes be muffled, or a hundred swords
Will storm his heart, Love's fev'rous citadel:
For him, those chambers held barbarian hordes,
Hyena foemen, and hot-blooded lords,
Whose very dogs would execrations howl
Against his lineage: not one breast affords
Him any mercy, in that mansion foul,
Save one old beldame, weak in body and in soul.

Ah, happy chance! the aged creature came,
Shuffling along with ivory-headed wand,
To where he stood, hid from the torch's flame,
Behind a broad half-pillar, far beyond
The sound of merriment and chorus bland:
He startled her; but soon she knew his face,
And grasp'd his fingers in her palsied hand,
Saying, 'Mercy, Porphyro! hie thee from this place;
They are all here to-night, the whole blood-thirsty race!

'Get hence! get hence! there's dwarfish Hildebrand;
He had a fever late, and in the fit
He cursed thee and thine, both house and land:
Then there's that old Lord Maurice, not a whit
More tame for his gray hairs – Alas me! flit!
Flit like a ghost away.' – 'Ah, Gossip dear,
We're safe enough; here in this arm-chair sit,
And tell me how' – 'Good Saints! not here, not here;
Follow me, child, or else these stones will be thy bier.'

He follow'd through a lowly arched way,
Brushing the cobwebs with his lofty plume,
And as she mutter'd 'Well-a – well-a-day!'
He found him in a little moonlight room,
Pale, lattic'd, chill, and silent as a tomb.
'Now tell me where is Madeline,' said he,
'O tell me, Angela, by the holy loom
Which none but secret sisterhood may see,
When they St. Agnes' wool are weaving piously.'

'St. Agnes! Ah! it is St. Agnes' Eve –
Yet men will murder upon holy days:
Thou must hold water in a witch's sieve,
And be liege-lord of all the Elves and Fays,
To venture so: it fills me with amaze
To see thee, Porphyro! – St. Agnes' Eve!
God's help! my lady fair the conjuror plays
This very night: good angels her deceive!
But let me laugh awhile, I've mickle time to grieve.'

Feebly she laugheth in the languid moon,
While Porphyro upon her face doth look,
Like puzzled urchin on an aged crone
Who keepeth clos'd a wond'rous riddle-book,
As spectacled she sits in chimney nook.
But soon his eyes grew brilliant, when she told
His lady's purpose; and he scarce could brook
Tears, at the thought of those enchantments cold,
And Madeline asleep in lap of legends old.

Sudden a thought came like a full-blown rose,
Flushing his brow, and in his pained heart
Made purple riot: then doth he propose
A stratagem, that makes the beldame start:
'A cruel man and impious thou art:
Sweet lady, let her pray, and sleep, and dream
Alone with her good angels, far apart
From wicked men like thee. Go, go! – I deem
Thou canst not surely be the same that thou didst seem.'

'I will not harm her, by all saints I swear,'
Quoth Porphyro: 'O may I ne'er find grace
When my weak voice shall whisper its last prayer,
If one of her soft ringlets I displace,
Or look with ruffian passion in her face:
Good Angela, believe me by these tears;
Or I will, even in a moment's space,
Awake, with horrid shout, my foemen's ears,
And beard them, though they be more fang'd than wolves
    and bears.'

'Ah! why wilt thou affright a feeble soul?
A poor, weak, palsy-stricken, churchyard thing,
Whose passing-bell may ere the midnight toll;
Whose prayers for thee, each morn and evening,
Were never miss'd.' – Thus plaining, doth she bring
A gentler speech from burning Porphyro;
So woful, and of such deep sorrowing,
That Angela gives promise she will do
Whatever he shall wish, betide her weal or woe.

Which was, to lead him, in close secrecy,
Even to Madeline's chamber, and there hide
Him in a closet, of such privacy
That he might see her beauty unespy'd,
And win perhaps that night a peerless bride,
While legion'd faeries pac'd the coverlet,
And pale enchantment held her sleepy-ey'd.
Never on such a night have lovers met,
Since Merlin paid his Demon all the monstrous debt.

'It shall be as thou wishest,' said the Dame:
'All cates and dainties shall be stored there
Quickly on this feast-night: by the tambour frame
Her own lute thou wilt see: no time to spare,
For I am slow and feeble, and scarce dare
On such a catering trust my dizzy head.
Wait here, my child, with patience; kneel in prayer
The while: Ah! thou must needs the lady wed,
Or may I never leave my grave among the dead.'

So saying, she hobbled off with busy fear.
The lover's endless minutes slowly pass'd;
The dame return'd, and whisper'd in his ear
To follow her; with aged eyes aghast
From fright of dim espial. Safe at last,
Through many a dusky gallery, they gain
The maiden's chamber, silken, hush'd, and chaste;
Where Porphyro took covert, pleas'd amain.
His poor guide hurried back with agues in her brain.

Her falt'ring hand upon the balustrade,
Old Angela was feeling for the stair,
When Madeline, St. Agnes' charmed maid,
Rose, like a mission'd spirit, unaware:
With silver taper's light, and pious care,
She turn'd, and down the aged gossip led
To a safe level matting. Now prepare,
Young Porphyro, for gazing on that bed;
She comes, she comes again, like ring-dove fray'd and fled.

Out went the taper as she hurried in;
Its little smoke, in pallid moonshine, died:
She clos'd the door, she panted, all akin
To spirits of the air, and visions wide:
No uttered syllable, or, woe betide!
But to her heart, her heart was voluble,
Paining with eloquence her balmy side;
As though a tongueless nightingale should swell
Her throat in vain, and die, heart-stifled, in her dell.

A casement high and triple-arch'd there was,
All garlanded with carven imag'ries
Of fruits, and flowers, and bunches of knot-grass,
And diamonded with panes of quaint device,
Innumerable of stains and splendid dyes,
As are the tiger-moth's deep-damask'd wings;
And in the midst, 'mong thousand heraldries,
And twilight saints, and dim emblazonings,
A shielded scutcheon blush'd with blood of queens
    and kings.

Full on this casement shone the wintry moon,

And threw warm gules on Madeline's fair breast,

As down she knelt for heaven's grace and boon;

Rose-bloom fell on her hands, together prest,

And on her silver cross soft amethyst,

And on her hair a glory, like a saint:

She seem'd a splendid angel, newly drest,

Save wings, for heaven: – Porphyro grew faint:

She knelt, so pure a thing, so free from mortal taint.

Anon his heart revives: her vespers done,

Of all its wreathed pearls her hair she frees;

Unclasps her warmed jewels one by one;

Loosens her fragrant boddice; by degrees

Her rich attire creeps rustling to her knees:

Half-hidden, like a mermaid in sea-weed,

Pensive awhile she dreams awake, and sees,

In fancy, fair St. Agnes in her bed,

But dares not look behind, or all the charm is fled.

Soon, trembling in her soft and chilly nest,

In sort of wakeful swoon, perplex'd she lay,

Until the poppied warmth of sleep oppress'd

Her soothed limbs, and soul fatigued away;

Flown, like a thought, until the morrow-day;

Blissfully haven'd both from joy and pain;

Clasp'd like a missal where swart Paynims pray;

Blinded alike from sunshine and from rain,

As though a rose should shut, and be a bud again.

Stol'n to this paradise, and so entranced,

Porphyro gaz'd upon her empty dress,

And listen'd to her breathing, if it chanced

To wake into a slumberous tenderness;

Which when he heard, that minute did he bless,

And breath'd himself: then from the closet crept,

Noiseless as fear in a wide wilderness,

And over the hush'd carpet, silent, stept,

And 'tween the curtains peep'd, where, lo! – how fast
she slept.

Then by the bed-side, where the faded moon
Made a dim, silver twilight, soft he set
A table, and, half anguish'd, threw thereon
A cloth of woven crimson, gold, and jet: –
O for some drowsy Morphean amulet!
The boisterous, midnight, festive clarion,
The kettle-drum, and far-heard clarinet,
Affray his ears, though but in dying tone: –
The hall door shuts again, and all the noise is gone.

And still she slept an azure-lidded sleep,
In blanched linen, smooth, and lavender'd,
While he forth from the closet brought a heap
Of candied apple, quince, and plum, and gourd;
With jellies soother than the creamy curd,
And lucent syrops, tinct with cinnamon;
Manna and dates, in argosy transferr'd
From Fez; and spiced dainties, every one,
From silken Samarcand to cedar'd Lebanon.

These delicates he heap'd with glowing hand
On golden dishes and in baskets bright
Of wreathed silver: sumptuous they stand
In the retired quiet of the night,
Filling the chilly room with perfume light. –
'And now, my love, my seraph fair, awake!
Thou art my heaven, and I thine eremite:
Open thine eyes, for meek St. Agnes' sake,
Or I shall drowse beside thee, so my soul doth ache.'

Thus whispering, his warm, unnerved arm
Sank in her pillow. Shaded was her dream
By the dusk curtains: – 'twas a midnight charm
Impossible to melt as iced stream:
The lustrous salvers in the moonlight gleam;
Broad golden fringe upon the carpet lies:
It seem'd he never, never could redeem
From such a stedfast spell his lady's eyes;
So mus'd awhile, entoil'd in woofed phantasies.

Awakening up, he took her hollow lute, –
Tumultuous, – and, in chords that tenderest be,
He play'd an ancient ditty, long since mute,
In Provence call'd, 'La belle dame sans mercy':
Close to her ear touching the melody; –
Wherewith disturb'd, she utter'd a soft moan:
He ceas'd – she panted quick – and suddenly
Her blue affrayed eyes wide open shone:
Upon his knees he sank, pale as smooth-sculptured stone.

Her eyes were open, but she still beheld,
Now wide awake, the vision of her sleep:
There was a painful change, that nigh expell'd
The blisses of her dream so pure and deep
At which fair Madeline began to weep,
And moan forth witless words with many a sigh;
While still her gaze on Porphyro would keep;
Who knelt, with joined hands and piteous eye,
Fearing to move or speak, she look'd so dreamingly.

'Ah, Porphyro!' said she, 'but even now
Thy voice was at sweet tremble in mine ear,
Made tuneable with every sweetest vow;
And those sad eyes were spiritual and clear:
How chang'd thou art! how pallid, chill, and drear!
Give me that voice again, my Porphyro,
Those looks immortal, those complainings dear!
Oh leave me not in this eternal woe,
For if thy diest, my Love, I know not where to go.'

Beyond a mortal man impassion'd far
At these voluptuous accents, he arose
Ethereal, flush'd, and like a throbbing star
Seen mid the sapphire heaven's deep repose;
Into her dream he melted, as the rose
Blendeth its odour with the violet, –
Solution sweet: meantime the frost-wind blows
Like Love's alarum pattering the sharp sleet
Against the window-panes; St. Agnes' moon hath set.

'Tis dark: quick pattereth the flaw-blown sleet:
'This is no dream, my bride, my Madeline!'
'Tis dark: the iced gusts still rave and beat:
'No dream, alas! alas! and woe is mine!
Porphyro will leave me here to fade and pine. –
Cruel! what traitor could thee hither bring?
I curse not, for my heart is lost in thine,
Though thou forsakest a deceived thing; –
A dove forlorn and lost with sick unpruned wing.'

'My Madeline! sweet dreamer! lovely bride!
Say, may I be for aye thy vassal blest?
Thy beauty's shield, heart-shap'd and vermeil dyed?
Ah, silver shrine, here will I take my rest
After so many hours of toil and quest,
A famish'd pilgrim, – sav'd by miracle.
Though I have found, I will not rob thy nest
Saving of thy sweet self; if thou think'st well
To trust, fair Madeline, to no rude infidel.

'Hark! 'tis an elfin-storm from faery land,
Of haggard seeming, but a boon indeed:
Arise – arise! the morning is at hand; –
The bloated wassaillers will never heed: –
Let us away, my love, with happy speed;
There are no ears to hear, or eyes to see, –
Drown'd all in Rhenish and the sleepy mead:
Awake! arise! my love, and fearless be,
For o'er the southern moors I have a home for thee.'

She hurried at his words, beset with fears,
For there were sleeping dragons all around,
At glaring watch, perhaps, with ready spears –
Down the wide stairs a darkling way they found. –
In all the house was heard no human sound.
A chain-droop'd lamp was flickering by each door;
The arras, rich with horseman, hawk, and hound,
Flutter'd in the besieging wind's uproar;
And the long carpets rose along the gusty floor.

They glide, like phantoms, into the wide hall;
Like phantoms, to the iron porch, they glide;
Where lay the Porter, in uneasy sprawl,
With a huge empty flaggon by his side:
The wakeful bloodhound rose, and shook his hide,
But his sagacious eye an inmate owns:
By one, and one, the bolts full easy slide: –
The chains lie silent on the footworn stones; –
The key turns, and the door upon its hinges groans.

And they are gone: ay, ages long ago
These lovers fled away into the storm.
That night the Baron dreamt of many a woe,
And all his warrior-guests, with shade and form
Of witch, and demon, and large coffin-worm,
Were long be-nightmar'd. Angela the old
Died palsy-twitch'd, with meagre face deform;
The Beadsman, after thousand aves told,
For aye unsought for slept among his ashes cold.

1819

On a Dream

As Hermes once took to his feathers light,
When lulled Argus, baffled, swoon'd and slept,
So on a Delphic reed, my idle spright
So play'd, so charm'd, so conquer'd, so bereft
The dragon-world of all its hundred eyes;
And seeing it asleep, so fled away,
Not to pure Ida with its snow-cold skies,
Nor unto Tempe where Jove griev'd that day;
But to that second circle of sad Hell,
Where in the gust, the whirlwind, and the flaw
Of rain and hail-stones, lovers need not tell
Their sorrows – pale were the sweet lips I saw,
Pale were the lips I kiss'd, and fair the form
I floated with, about that melancholy storm.

1819

To Sleep

O soft embalmer of the still midnight!
Shutting, with careful fingers and benign,
Our gloom-pleas'd eyes, embower'd from the light,
Enshaded in forgetfulness divine:
O soothest Sleep! if so it please thee, close
In midst of this thine hymn my willing eyes,
Or wait the 'Amen', ere thy poppy throws
Around my bed its lulling charities.
Then save me, or the passed day will shine
Upon my pillow, breeding many woes, –
Save me from curious Conscience, that still lords
Its strength for darkness, burrowing like a mole;
Turn the key deftly in the oiled wards,
And seal the hushed Casket of my Soul.

1819

ODE TO PSYCHE

O Goddess! hear these tuneless numbers, wrung

By sweet enforcement and remembrance dear,

And pardon that thy secrets should be sung

Even into thine own soft-conched ear:

Surely I dreamt to-day, or did I see

The winged Psyche with awaken'd eyes?

I wander'd in a forest thoughtlessly,

And, on the sudden, fainting with surprise,

Saw two fair creatures, couched side by side

In deepest grass, beneath the whisp'ring roof

Of leaves and trembled blossoms, where there ran

A brooklet, scarce espied:

Mid hush'd, cool-rooted flowers, fragrant-eyed,

Blue, silver-white, and budded Tyrian,

They lay calm-breathing, on the bedded grass;

Their arms embraced, and their pinions too;

Their lips touch'd not, but had not bade adieu,

As if disjoined by soft-handed slumber,

And ready still past kisses to outnumber

At tender eye-dawn of aurorean love:

The winged boy I knew;
But who wast thou, O happy, happy dove?
His Psyche true!

O latest born and loveliest vision far
Of all Olympus' faded hierarchy!
Fairer than Phoebe's sapphire-region'd star,
Or Vesper, amorous glow-worm of the sky;
Fairer than these, though temple thou hast none,
Nor altar heap'd with flowers;
Nor virgin-choir to make delicious moan
Upon the midnight hours;
No voice, no lute, no pipe, no incense sweet
From chain-swung censer teeming;
No shrine, no grove, no oracle, no heat
Of pale-mouth'd prophet dreaming.

O brightest! though too late for antique vows,
Too, too late for the fond believing lyre,
When holy were the haunted forest boughs,
Holy the air, the water, and the fire;
Yet even in these days so far retir'd
From happy pieties, thy lucent fans,

Fluttering among the faint Olympians,
I see, and sing, by my own eyes inspir'd.
So let me be thy choir, and make a moan
Upon the midnight hours;
Thy voice, thy lute, thy pipe, thy incense sweet
From swinged censer teeming;
Thy shrine, thy grove, thy oracle, thy heat
Of pale-mouth'd prophet dreaming.

Yes, I will be thy priest, and build a fane
In some untrodden region of my mind,
Where branched thoughts, new grown with pleasant pain,
Instead of pines shall murmur in the wind:
Far, far around shall those dark-cluster'd trees
Fledge the wild-ridged mountains steep by steep;
And there by zephyrs, streams, and birds, and bees,
The moss-lain Dryads shall be lull'd to sleep;
And in the midst of this wide quietness
A rosy sanctuary will I dress
With the wreath'd trellis of a working brain,
With buds, and bells, and stars without a name,
With all the gardener Fancy e'er could feign,
Who breeding flowers, will never breed the same:

And there shall be for thee all soft delight
That shadowy thought can win,
A bright torch, and a casement ope at night,
To let the warm Love in!

1819

ODE TO A NIGHTINGALE

My heart aches, and a drowsy numbness pains
My sense, as though of hemlock I had drunk,
Or emptied some dull opiate to the drains
One minute past, and Lethe-wards had sunk:
'Tis not through envy of thy happy lot,
But being too happy in thine happiness, –
That thou, light-winged Dryad of the trees
    In some melodious plot
Of beechen green, and shadows numberless,
Singest of summer in full-throated ease.

O, for a draught of vintage! that hath been
Cool'd a long age in the deep-delved earth,
Tasting of Flora and the country green,
Dance, and Provençal song, and sunburnt mirth!
O for a beaker full of the warm South,
Full of the true, the blushful Hippocrene,
With beaded bubbles winking at the brim,
    And purple-stained mouth;
That I might drink, and leave the world unseen,
And with thee fade away into the forest dim:

Fade far away, dissolve, and quite forget
What thou among the leaves hast never known,
The weariness, the fever, and the fret
Here, where men sit and hear each other groan;
Where palsy shakes a few, sad, last gray hairs,
Where youth grows pale, and spectre-thin, and dies;
Where but to think is to be full of sorrow
And leaden-eyed despairs,
Where Beauty cannot keep her lustrous eyes,
Or new Love pine at them beyond to-morrow.

Away! away! for I will fly to thee,
Not charioted by Bacchus and his pards,
But on the viewless wings of Poesy,
Though the dull brain perplexes and retards:
Already with thee! tender is the night,
And haply the Queen-Moon is on her throne,
Cluster'd around by all her starry Fays;
But here there is no light,
Save what from heaven is with the breezes blown
Through verdurous glooms and winding mossy ways.

I cannot see what flowers are at my feet,
Nor what soft incense hangs upon the boughs,
But, in embalmed darkness, guess each sweet
Wherewith the seasonable month endows
The grass, the thicket, and the fruit-tree wild;
White hawthorn, and the pastoral eglantine;
Fast fading violets cover'd up in leaves;
And mid-May's eldest child,
The coming musk-rose, full of dewy wine,
The murmurous haunt of flies on summer eves.

Darkling I listen; and, for many a time
I have been half in love with easeful Death,
Call'd him soft names in many a mused rhyme,
To take into the air my quiet breath;
Now more than ever seems it rich to die,
To cease upon the midnight with no pain,
While thou art pouring forth thy soul abroad
In such an ecstasy!
Still wouldst thou sing, and I have ears in vain –
To thy high requiem become a sod.

Thou wast not born for death, immortal Bird!
No hungry generations tread thee down;
The voice I hear this passing night was heard
In ancient days by emperor and clown:
Perhaps the self-same song that found a path
Through the sad heart of Ruth, when, sick for home,
She stood in tears amid the alien corn;
The same that oft-times hath
Charm'd magic casements, opening on the foam
Of perilous seas, in faery lands forlorn.

Forlorn! the very word is like a bell
To toll me back from thee to my sole self!
Adieu! the fancy cannot cheat so well
As she is fam'd to do, deceiving elf.
Adieu! adieu! thy plaintive anthem fades
Past the near meadows, over the still stream,
Up the hill-side; and now 'tis buried deep
In the next valley-glades:
Was it a vision, or a waking dream?
Fled is that music: – Do I wake or sleep?

ODE ON MELANCHOLY

No, no, go not to Lethe, neither twist
Wolf's-bane, tight-rooted, for its poisonous wine;
Nor suffer thy pale forehead to be kiss'd
By nightshade, ruby grape of Proserpine;
Make not your rosary of yew-berries,
Nor let the beetle, nor the death-moth be
Your mournful Psyche, nor the downy owl
A partner in your sorrow's mysteries;
For shade to shade will come too drowsily,
 And drown the wakeful anguish of the soul.

But when the melancholy fit shall fall
Sudden from heaven like a weeping cloud,
That fosters the droop-headed flowers all,
And hides the green hill in an April shroud;
Then glut thy sorrow on a morning rose,
Or on the rainbow of the salt sand-wave,
Or on the wealth of globed peonies;
Or if thy mistress some rich anger shows,
Emprison her soft hand, and let her rave,
And feed deep, deep upon her peerless eyes.

She dwells with Beauty – Beauty that must die;
And Joy, whose hand is ever at his lips
Bidding adieu; and aching Pleasure nigh,
Turning to poison while the bee-mouth sips:
Ay, in the very temple of Delight
Veil'd Melancholy has her sovran shrine,
Though seen of none save him whose strenuous tongue
Can burst Joy's grape against his palate fine;
His soul shalt taste the sadness of her might,
And be among her cloudy trophies hung.

1819

ODE ON INDOLENCE

'They toil not, neither do they spin.'

One morn before me were three figures seen,
With bowèd necks, and joinèd hands, side-faced;
And one behind the other stepp'd serene,
 In placid sandals, and in white robes graced;
They pass'd, like figures on a marble urn,
When shifted round to see the other side;
They came again; as when the urn once more
Is shifted round, the first seen shades return;
And they were strange to me, as may betide
With vases, to one deep in Phidian lore.

How is it, Shadows! that I knew ye not?
How came ye muffled in so hush a mask?
Was it a silent deep-disguised plot
To steal away, and leave without a task
My idle days? Ripe was the drowsy hour;
The blissful cloud of summer-indolence
Benumb'd my eyes; my pulse grew less and less;
Pain had no sting, and pleasure's wreath no flower:
O, why did ye not melt, and leave my sense

Unhaunted quite of all but – nothingness?

A third time pass'd they by, and, passing, turn'd
Each one the face a moment whiles to me;
Then faded, and to follow them I burn'd
And ached for wings, because I knew the three;
The first was a fair Maid, and Love her name;
The second was Ambition, pale of cheek,
And ever watchful with fatigued eye;
The last, whom I love more, the more of blame
Is heap'd upon her, maiden most unmeek, –
I knew to be my demon Poesy.

They faded, and, forsooth! I wanted wings:
O folly! What is Love? and where is it?
And for that poor Ambition! it springs
From a man's little heart's short fever-fit;
For Poesy! – no, – she has not a joy, –
At least for me, – so sweet as drowsy noons,
And evenings steep'd in honey'd indolence;
O, for an age so shelter'd from annoy,
That I may never know how change the moons,
Or hear the voice of busy common-sense!

And once more came they by: – alas! wherefore?
My sleep had been embroider'd with dim dreams;
My soul had been a lawn besprinkled o'er
With flowers, and stirring shades, and baffled beams:
The morn was clouded, but no shower fell,
Tho' in her lids hung the sweet tears of May;
The open casement press'd a new-leaved vine,
Let in the budding warmth and throstle's lay;
O Shadows! 'twas a time to bid farewell!
Upon your skirts had fallen no tears of mine.

So, ye three Ghosts, adieu! Ye cannot raise
My head cool-bedded in the flowery grass;
For I would not be dieted with praise,
A pet-lamb in a sentimental farce!
Fade softly from my eyes, and be once more
 In masque-like figures on the dreamy urn;
Farewell! I yet have visions for the night,
And for the day faint visions there is store;
Vanish, ye Phantoms! from my idle spright,
Into the clouds, and never more return!

1819

THE FALL OF HYPERION (EXTRACT)

Methought I stood where trees of every clime,
Palm, myrtle, oak, and sycamore, and beech,
With Plantane, and spice blossoms, made a screen;
In neighbourhood of fountains, by the noise
Soft showering in my ears, and, by the touch
Of scent, not far from roses. Turning round
I saw an arbour with a drooping roof
Of trellis vines, and bells, and larger blooms,
Like floral censers swinging light in air;
Before its wreathed doorway, on a mound
Of moss, was spread a feast of summer fruits,
Which, nearer seen, seem'd refuse of a meal
By angel tasted or our Mother Eve;
For empty shells were scattered on the grass,
And grape stalks but half bare, and remnants more,
Sweet smelling, whose pure kinds I could not know.
Still was more plenty than the fabled horn
Thrice emptied could pour forth, at banqueting
For Proserpine return'd to her own fields,
Where the white heifers low. And appetite
More yearning than on earth I ever felt

Growing within, I ate deliciously;
And, after not long, thirsted, for thereby
Stood a cool vessel of transparent juice
Sipp'd by the wander'd bee, the which I took,
And, pledging all the mortals of the world,
And all the dead whose names are in our lips,
Drank. That full draught is parent of my theme.
No Asian poppy nor elixir fine
Of the soon fading jealous Caliphat,
No poison gender'd in close monkish cell
To thin the scarlet conclave of old men,
Could so have rapt unwilling life away.
Among the fragrant husks and berries crush'd,
Upon the grass I struggled hard against
The domineering potion; but in vain:
The cloudy swoon came on, and down I sunk
Like a Silenus on an antique vase.
How long I slumber'd 'tis a chance to guess.
When sense of life return'd, I started up
As if with wings; but the fair trees were gone,
The mossy mound and arbour were no more:
I look'd around upon the carved sides
Of an old sanctuary with roof august,

Builded so high, it seem'd that filmed clouds
Might spread beneath, as o'er the stars of heaven;
So old the place was, I remember'd none
The like upon the earth: what I had seen
Of grey cathedrals, buttress'd walls, rent towers,
The superannuations of sunk realms,
Or Nature's rocks toil'd hard in waves and winds,
Seem'd but the faulture of decrepit things
To that eternal domed monument.
Upon the marble at my feet there lay
Store of strange vessels and large draperies,
Which needs had been of dyed asbestos wove,
Or in that place the moth could not corrupt,
So white the linen, so, in some, distinct
Ran imageries from a sombre loom.
All in a mingled heap confus'd there lay
Robes, golden tongs, censer and chafing dish,
Girdles, and chains, and holy jewelries.

1819

ON LOVE
& FRIENDSHIP

Wherein Lies Happiness?

FILL FOR ME A BRIMMING BOWL

Fill for me a brimming bowl
And in it let me drown my soul:
But put therein some drug, designed
To Banish Women from my mind:
For I want not the stream inspiring
That fills the mind with – fond desiring,
But I want as deep a draught
As e'er from Lethe's wave was quaff'd;
From my despairing heart to charm
The Image of the fairest form
That e'er my reveling eyes beheld,
That e'er my wandering fancy spell'd.
In vain! away I cannot chace
The melting softness of that face,
The beaminess of those bright eyes,
That breast – earth's only Paradise.
My sight will never more be blest;
For all I see has lost its zest:
Nor with delight can I explore,
The Classic page, or Muse's lore.
Had she but known how beat my heart,

And with one smile reliev'd its smart
I should have felt a sweet relief,
I should have felt 'the joy of grief'.
Yet as the Tuscan mid the snow
Of Lapland dreams on sweet Arno,
Even so for ever shall she be
The Halo of my Memory.

1814

Written on the Day that Mr. Leigh Hunt Left Prison

What though, for showing truth to flatter'd state,
Kind Hunt was shut in prison, yet has he,
In his immortal spirit, been as free
As the sky-searching lark, and as elate.
Minion of grandeur! think you he did wait?
Think you he nought but prison walls did see,
Till, so unwilling, thou unturn'dst the key?
Ah, no! far happier, nobler was his fate!
In Spenser's halls he strayed, and bowers fair,
Culling enchanted flowers; and he flew
With daring Milton through the fields of air:
To regions of his own his genius true
Took happy flights. Who shall his fame impair
When thou art dead, and all thy wretched crew?

1815

TO HOPE

When by my solitary hearth I sit,
And hateful thoughts enwrap my soul in gloom;
When no fair dreams before my 'mind's eye' flit,
And the bare heath of life presents no bloom;
Sweet Hope, ethereal balm upon me shed,
And wave thy silver pinions o'er my head!

Whene'er I wander, at the fall of night,
Where woven boughs shut out the moon's bright ray,
Should sad Despondency my musings fright,
And frown, to drive fair Cheerfulness away,
Peep with the moonbeams through the leafy roof,
And keep that fiend Despondence far aloof!

Should Disappointment, parent of Despair,
Strive for her son to seize my careless heart;
When, like a cloud, he sits upon the air,
Preparing on his spell-bound prey to dart:
Chase him away, sweet Hope, with visage bright,
And fright him as the morning frightens night!
Whene'er the fate of those I hold most dear

Tells to my fearful breast a tale of sorrow,
O bright-eyed Hope, my morbid fancy cheer;
Let me awhile thy sweetest comforts borrow:
Thy heaven-born radiance around me shed,
And wave thy silver pinions o'er my head!

Should e'er unhappy love my bosom pain,
From cruel parents, or relentless fair;
O let me think it is not quite in vain
To sigh out sonnets to the midnight air!
Sweet Hope, ethereal balm upon me shed,
And wave thy silver pinions o'er my head!

In the long vista of the years to roll,
Let me not see our country's honour fade:
O let me see our land retain her soul,
Her pride, her freedom; and not freedom's shade.
From thy bright eyes unusual brightness shed
Beneath thy pinions canopy my head!

Let me not see the patriot's high bequest,
Great Liberty! how great in plain attire!
With the base purple of a court oppress'd,

Bowing her head, and ready to expire:
But let me see thee stoop from heaven on wings
That fill the skies with silver glitterings!

And as, in sparkling majesty, a star
Gilds the bright summit of some gloomy cloud;
Brightening the half veil'd face of heaven afar:
So, when dark thoughts my boding spirit shroud,
Sweet Hope, celestial influence round me shed,
Waving thy silver pinions o'er my head!

1815

To. . .

Had I a man's fair form, then might my sighs
Be echoed swiftly through that ivory shell
Thine ear, and find thy gentle heart; so well
Would passion arm me for the enterprise;
But ah! I am no knight whose foeman dies;
No cuirass glistens on my bosom's swell;
I am no happy shepherd of the dell
Whose lips have trembled with a maiden's eyes.
Yet must I dote upon thee – call thee sweet,
Sweeter by far than Hybla's honied roses
When steep'd in dew rich to intoxication.
Ah! I will taste that dew, for me 'tis meet,
And when the moon her pallid face discloses,
I'll gather some by spells, and incantation.

1816

To a Young Lady who Sent Me a Laurel Crown

Fresh morning gusts have blown away all fear
From my glad bosom – now from gloominess
I mount forever – not an atom less
Than the proud laurel shall content my bier.
No! by the eternal stars! or why sit here
In the Sun's eye, and 'gainst my temples press
Apollo's very leaves, woven to bless
By thy white fingers and thy spirit clear.
Lo! who dares say, Do this? Who dares call down
My will from its high purpose? Who say, 'Stand',
Or 'Go'? This mighty moment I would frown
On abject Caesars – not the stoutest band
Of mailed heroes should tear off my crown:
Yet would I kneel and kiss thy gentle hand!

1816

TO HAYDON

Great spirits now on earth are sojourning;
He of the cloud, the cataract, the lake,
Who on Helvellyn's summit, wide awake,
Catches his freshness from Archangel's wing;
He of the rose, the violet, the spring,
The social smile, the chain for Freedom's sake:
And lo! – whose steadfastness would never take
A meaner sound than Raphael's whispering.
And other spirits there are standing apart
Upon the forehead of the age to come;
These, these will give the world another heart
And other pulses. Hear ye not the hum
Of mighty workings in the human mart?
Listen awhile, ye nations, and be dumb.

1816

SLEEP AND POETRY (EXTRACT)

As I lay in my bed slepe full unmete
Was unto me, but why that I ne might
Rest I ne wist, for there n'as erthly wight
[As I suppose] had more of hertis ese
Than I, for I n'ad sicknesse nor disese.
Chaucer

O for ten years, that I may overwhelm
Myself in poesy; so I may do the deed
That my own soul has to itself decreed.
Then I will pass the countries that I see
In long perspective, and continually
Taste their pure fountains. First the realm I'll pass
Of Flora, and old Pan: sleep in the grass,
Feed upon apples red, and strawberries,
And choose each pleasure that my fancy sees;
Catch the white-handed nymphs in shady places,
To woo sweet kisses from averted faces, –
Play with their fingers, touch their shoulders white
Into a pretty shrinking with a bite
As hard as lips can make it: till agreed,

A lovely tale of human life we'll read.
And one will teach a tame dove how it best
May fan the cool air gently o'er my rest;
Another, bending o'er her nimble tread,
Will set a green robe floating round her head,
And still will dance with ever varied ease,
Smiling upon the flowers and the trees:
Another will entice me on, and on
Through almond blossoms and rich cinnamon,
Till in the bosom of a leafy world
We rest in silence, like two gems upcurl'd
In the recesses of a pearly shell.

And can I ever bid these joys farewell?
Yes, I must pass them for a nobler life,
Where I may find the agonies, the strife
Of human hearts: for lo! I see afar,
O'er sailing the blue cragginess, a car
And steeds with streamy manes – the charioteer
Looks out upon the winds with glorious fear:
And now the numerous tramplings quiver lightly
Along a huge cloud's ridge; and now with sprightly
Wheel downward come they into fresher skies,

Tipt round with silver from the sun's bright eyes.
Still downward with capacious whirl they glide;
And now I see them on a green-hill's side
In breezy rest among the nodding stalks.
The charioteer with wond'rous gesture talks
To the trees and mountains; and there soon appear
Shapes of delight, of mystery, and fear,
Passing along before a dusky space
Made by some mighty oaks: as they would chase
Some ever-fleeting music on they sweep.
Lo! how they murmur, laugh, and smile, and weep:
Some with upholden hand and mouth severe;
Some with their faces muffled to the ear
Between their arms; some, clear in youthful bloom,
Go glad and smilingly athwart the gloom;
Some looking back, and some with upward gaze;
Yes, thousands in a thousand different ways
Flit onward – now a lovely wreath of girls
Dancing their sleek hair into tangled curls;
And now broad wings. Most awfully intent
The driver of those steeds is forward bent,
And seems to listen: O that I might know
All that he writes with such a hurrying glow.

The visions all are fled – the car is fled
Into the light of heaven, and in their stead
A sense of real things comes doubly strong,
And, like a muddy stream, would bear along
My soul to nothingness: but I will strive
Against all doubtings, and will keep alive
The thought of that same chariot, and the strange
Journey it went.

1816

To Koscuisko

Good Kosciusko, thy great name alone
Is a full harvest whence to reap high feeling;
It comes upon us like the glorious pealing
Of the wide spheres – an everlasting tone.
And now it tells me, that in worlds unknown,
The names of heroes, burst from clouds concealing,
And changed to harmonies, for ever stealing
Through cloudless blue, and round each silver throne.
It tells me too, that on a happy day,
When some good spirit walks upon the earth,
Thy name with Alfred's, and the great of yore
Gently commingling, gives tremendous birth
To a loud hymn, that sounds far, far away
To where the great God lives for evermore.

1816

To Leigh Hunt, Esq.

Glory and loveliness have passed away;
For if we wander out in early morn,
No wreathed incense do we see upborne
Into the east, to meet the smiling day:
No crowd of nymphs soft voic'd and young, and gay,
In woven baskets bringing ears of corn,
Roses, and pinks, and violets, to adorn
The shrine of Flora in her early May.
But there are left delights as high as these,
And I shall ever bless my destiny,
That in a time, when under pleasant trees
Pan is no longer sought, I feel a free
A leafy luxury, seeing I could please
With these poor offerings, a man like thee.

1817

LINES

Unfelt unheard, unseen,
I've left my little queen,
Her languid arms in silver slumber lying:
Ah! through their nestling touch,
Who – who could tell how much
There is for madness – cruel, or complying?

Those faery lids how sleek!
Those lips how moist! – they speak,
In ripest quiet, shadows of sweet sounds:
Into my fancy's ear
Melting a burden dear,
How 'Love doth know no fulness, nor no bounds.'

True! – tender monitors!
I bend unto your laws:
This sweetest day for dalliance was born!
So, without more ado,
I'll feel my heaven anew,
For all the blushing of the hasty morn.

1817

To J. H. Reynolds

O that a week could be an age, and we
Felt parting and warm meeting every week,
Then one poor year a thousand years would be,
The flush of welcome ever on the cheek:
So could we live long life in little space,
So time itself would be annihilate,
So a day's journey in oblivious haze
To serve our joys would lengthen and dilate.
O to arrive each Monday morn from Ind!
To land each Tuesday from the rich Levant!
In little time a host of joys to bind,
And keep our souls in one eternal pant!
This morn, my friend, and yester-evening taught
Me how to harbour such a happy thought.

1818

ENDYMION (EXTRACT, BOOK I)

Wherein lies happiness? In that which becks
Our ready minds to fellowship divine,
A fellowship with essence; till we shine,
Full alchemiz'd, and free of space. Behold
The clear religion of heaven! Fold
A rose leaf round thy finger's taperness,
And soothe thy lips: hist, when the airy stress
Of music's kiss impregnates the free winds,
And with a sympathetic touch unbinds
Eolian magic from their lucid wombs:
Then old songs waken from enclouded tombs;
Old ditties sigh above their father's grave;
Ghosts of melodious prophesyings rave
Round every spot where trod Apollo's foot;
Bronze clarions awake, and faintly bruit,
Where long ago a giant battle was;
And, from the turf, a lullaby doth pass
In every place where infant Orpheus slept.
Feel we these things? – that moment have we stept
Into a sort of oneness, and our state
Is like a floating spirit's. But there are
Richer entanglements, enthralments far

More self-destroying, leading, by degrees,
To the chief intensity: the crown of these
Is made of love and friendship, and sits high
Upon the forehead of humanity.
All its more ponderous and bulky worth
Is friendship, whence there ever issues forth
A steady splendour; but at the tip-top,
There hangs by unseen film, an orbed drop
Of light, and that is love: its influence,
Thrown in our eyes, genders a novel sense,
At which we start and fret; till in the end,
Melting into its radiance, we blend,
Mingle, and so become a part of it, –
Nor with aught else can our souls interknit
So wingedly: when we combine therewith,
Life's self is nourish'd by its proper pith,
And we are nurtured like a pelican brood.
Aye, so delicious is the unsating food,
That men, who might have tower'd in the van
Of all the congregated world, to fan
And winnow from the coming step of time
All chaff of custom, wipe away all slime
Left by men-slugs and human serpentry,
Have been content to let occasion die,

Whilst they did sleep in love's elysium.
And, truly, I would rather be struck dumb,
Than speak against this ardent listlessness:
For I have ever thought that it might bless
The world with benefits unknowingly;
As does the nightingale, upperched high,
And cloister'd among cool and bunched leaves –
She sings but to her love, nor e'er conceives
How tiptoe Night holds back her dark-grey hood.
Just so may love, although 'tis understood
The mere commingling of passionate breath,
Produce more than our searching witnesseth:
What I know not: but who, of men, can tell
That flowers would bloom, or that green fruit would swell
To melting pulp, that fish would have bright mail,
The earth its dower of river, wood, and vale,
The meadows runnels, runnels pebble-stones,
The seed its harvest, or the lute its tones,
Tones ravishment, or ravishment its sweet,
If human souls did never kiss and greet?

1818

Lines on the Mermaid Tavern

Souls of Poets dead and gone,
What Elysium have ye known,
Happy field or mossy cavern,
Choicer than the Mermaid Tavern?
Have ye tippled drink more fine
Than mine host's Canary wine?
Or are fruits of Paradise
Sweeter than those dainty pies
Of venison? O generous food!
Drest as though bold Robin Hood
Would, with his maid Marian,
Sup and bowse from horn and can.

I have heard that on a day
Mine host's sign-board flew away,
Nobody knew whither, till
An astrologer's old quill
To a sheepskin gave the story,
Said he saw you in your glory,
Underneath a new old sign
Sipping beverage divine,

And pledging with contented smack
The Mermaid in the Zodiac.

Souls of Poets dead and gone,
What Elysium have ye known,
Happy field or mossy cavern,
Choicer than the Mermaid Tavern?

1818

Robin Hood

No! those days are gone away
And their hours are old and gray,
And their minutes buried all
Under the down-trodden pall
Of the leaves of many years:
Many times have winter's shears,
Frozen North, and chilling East,
Sounded tempests to the feast
Of the forest's whispering fleeces,
Since men knew nor rent nor leases.

No, the bugle sounds no more,
And the twanging bow no more;
Silent is the ivory shrill
Past the heath and up the hill;
There is no mid-forest laugh,
Where lone Echo gives the half
To some wight, amaz'd to hear
Jesting, deep in forest drear.

On the fairest time of June
You may go, with sun or moon,

Or the seven stars to light you,
Or the polar ray to right you;
But you never may behold
Little John, or Robin bold;
Never one, of all the clan,
Thrumming on an empty can
Some old hunting ditty, while
He doth his green way beguile
To fair hostess Merriment,
Down beside the pasture Trent;
For he left the merry tale
Messenger for spicy ale.

Gone, the merry morris din;
Gone, the song of Gamelyn;
Gone, the tough-belted outlaw
Idling in the 'grenè shawe';
All are gone away and past!
And if Robin should be cast
Sudden from his turfed grave,
And if Marian should have
Once again her forest days,
She would weep, and he would craze:

He would swear, for all his oaks,
Fall'n beneath the dockyard strokes,
Have rotted on the briny seas;
She would weep that her wild bees
Sang not to her – strange! that honey
Can't be got without hard money!

So it is: yet let us sing,
Honour to the old bow-string!
Honour to the bugle-horn!
Honour to the woods unshorn!
Honour to the Lincoln green!
Honour to the archer keen!
Honour to tight little John,
And the horse he rode upon!
Honour to bold Robin Hood,
Sleeping in the underwood!
Honour to maid Marian,
And to all the Sherwood-clan!
Though their days have hurried by
Let us two a burden try.

1818

To A Lady Seen For A Few Moments At Vauxhall

Time's sea hath been five years at its slow ebb,
Long hours have to and fro let creep the sand,
Since I was tangled in thy beauty's web,
And snared by the ungloving of thine hand.
And yet I never look on midnight sky,
But I behold thine eyes' well memory'd light;
I cannot look upon the rose's dye,
But to thy cheek my soul doth take its flight.
I cannot look on any budding flower,
But my fond ear, in fancy at thy lips
And hearkening for a love-sound, doth devour
Its sweets in the wrong sense: Thou dost eclipse
Every delight with sweet remembering,
And grief unto my darling joys dost bring.

1818

SONNET TO SPENSER

Spenser! a jealous honourer of thine,
A forester deep in thy midmost trees,
Did last eve ask my promise to refine
Some English that might strive thine ear to please.
But Elfin Poet 'tis impossible
For an inhabitant of wintry earth
To rise like Phoebus with a golden quill
Fire-wing'd and make a morning in his mirth.
It is impossible to escape from toil
O' the sudden and receive thy spiriting:
The flower must drink the nature of the soil
Before it can put forth its blossoming:
Be with me in the summer days, and I
Will for thine honour and his pleasure try.

1818

What the Thrush Said

O thou whose face hath felt the Winter's wind,
Whose eye has seen the snow-clouds hung in mist
And the black elm tops 'mong the freezing stars,
To thee the spring will be a harvest-time.
O thou, whose only book has been the light
Of supreme darkness which thou feddest on
Night after night when Phoebus was away,
To thee the Spring shall be a triple morn.
O fret not after knowledge – I have none,
And yet my song comes native with the warmth.
O fret not after knowledge – I have none,
And yet the Evening listens. He who saddens
At thought of idleness cannot be idle,
And he's awake who thinks himself asleep.

1818

Song

The stranger lighted from his steed,
And ere he spake a word,
He seiz'd my lady's lily hand,
And kiss'd it all unheard.

The stranger walk'd into the hall,
And ere he spake a word,
He kiss'd my lady's cherry lips,
And kiss'd 'em all unheard.

The stranger walk'd into the bower,
But my lady first did go,
Aye hand in hand into the bower,
Where my lord's roses blow.

My lady's maid had a silken scarf,
And a golden ring had she,
And a kiss from the stranger, as off he went
Again on his fair palfrey.

1818

Isabella; or, The Pot of Basil

A Story from Boccaccio

Fair Isabel, poor simple Isabel!
Lorenzo, a young palmer in Love's eye!
They could not in the self-same mansion dwell
Without some stir of heart, some malady;
They could not sit at meals but feel how well
It soothed each to be the other by;
They could not, sure, beneath the same roof sleep
But to each other dream, and nightly weep.

With every morn their love grew tenderer,
With every eve deeper and tenderer still;
He might not in house, field, or garden stir,
But her full shape would all his seeing fill;
And his continual voice was pleasanter
To her, than noise of trees or hidden rill;
Her lute-string gave an echo of his name,
She spoilt her half-done broidery with the same.

He knew whose gentle hand was at the latch,
Before the door had given her to his eyes;

And from her chamber-window he would catch
Her beauty farther than the falcon spies;
And constant as her vespers would he watch,
Because her face was turn'd to the same skies;
And with sick longing all the night outwear,
To hear her morning-step upon the stair.

A whole long month of May in this sad plight
Made their cheeks paler by the break of June:
'To morrow will I bow to my delight,
'To-morrow will I ask my lady's boon.' –
'O may I never see another night,
'Lorenzo, if thy lips breathe not love's tune.' –
So spake they to their pillows; but, alas,
Honeyless days and days did he let pass;

Until sweet Isabella's untouch'd cheek
Fell sick within the rose's just domain,
Fell thin as a young mother's, who doth seek
By every lull to cool her infant's pain:
'How ill she is,' said he, 'I may not speak,
'And yet I will, and tell my love all plain:
'If looks speak love-laws, I will drink her tears,

'And at the least 'twill startle off her cares.'

So said he one fair morning, and all day
His heart beat awfully against his side;
And to his heart he inwardly did pray
For power to speak; but still the ruddy tide
Stifled his voice, and puls'd resolve away –
Fever'd his high conceit of such a bride,
Yet brought him to the meekness of a child:
Alas! when passion is both meek and wild!

So once more he had wak'd and anguished
A dreary night of love and misery,
If Isabel's quick eye had not been wed
To every symbol on his forehead high;
She saw it waxing very pale and dead,
And straight all flush'd; so, lisped tenderly,
'Lorenzo!' – here she ceas'd her timid quest,
But in her tone and look he read the rest.

'O Isabella, I can half perceive
'That I may speak my grief into thine ear;
'If thou didst ever any thing believe,

'Believe how I love thee, believe how near
'My soul is to its doom: I would not grieve
'Thy hand by unwelcome pressing, would not fear
'Thine eyes by gazing; but I cannot live
'Another night, and not my passion shrive.

'Love! thou art leading me from wintry cold,
'Lady! thou leadest me to summer clime,
'And I must taste the blossoms that unfold
'In its ripe warmth this gracious morning time.'
So said, his erewhile timid lips grew bold,
And poesied with hers in dewy rhyme:
Great bliss was with them, and great happiness
Grew, like a lusty flower in June's caress.

1818

WHERE'S THE POET?

Where's the Poet? show him! show him,
Muses nine! that I may know him.
'Tis the man who with a man
Is an equal, be he King,
Or poorest of the beggar-clan
Or any other wonderous thing
A man may be 'twixt ape and Plato;
'Tis the man who with a bird,
Wren or Eagle, finds his way to
All its instincts; he hath heard
The Lion's roaring, and can tell
What his horny throat expresseth,
And to him the Tiger's yell
Come articulate and presseth
Or his ear like mother-tongue.

1818

Modern Love

And what is love? It is a doll dress'd up
For idleness to cosset, nurse, and dandle;
A thing of soft misnomers, so divine
That silly youth doth think to make itself
Divine by loving, and so goes on
Yawning and doting a whole summer long,
Till Miss's comb is made a pearl tiara,
And common Wellingtons turn Romeo boots;
Then Cleopatra lives at number seven,
And Antony resides in Brunswick Square.
Fools! if some passions high have warm'd the world,
If Queens and Soldiers have play'd deep for hearts,
It is no reason why such agonies
Should be more common than the growth of weeds.
Fools! make me whole again that weighty pearl
The Queen of Egypt melted, and I'll say
That ye may love in spite of beaver hats.

1818

BARDS OF PASSION & MIRTH

Bards of Passion and of Mirth,
Ye have left your souls on earth!
Have ye souls in heaven too,
Doubled-lived in regions new?
Yes, and those of heaven commune
With the spheres of sun and moon;
With the noise of fountains wondrous,
And the parle of voices thund'rous;
With the whisper of heaven's trees
And one another, in soft ease
Seated on Elysian lawns
Browsed by none but Dian's fawns;
Underneath large blue-bells tented,
Where the daisies are rose-scented,
And the rose herself has got
Perfume which on earth is not;
Where the nightingale doth sing
Not a senseless, tranced thing,
But divine melodious truth;
Philosophic numbers smooth;
Tales and golden histories
Of heaven and its mysteries.

Thus ye live on high, and then
On the earth ye live again;
And the souls ye left behind you
Teach us, here, the way to find you,
Where your other souls are joying,
Never slumber'd, never cloying.
Here, your earth-born souls still speak
To mortals, of their little week;
Of their sorrows and delights;
Of their passions and their spites;
Of their glory and their shame;
What doth strengthen and what maim.
Thus ye teach us, every day,
Wisdom, though fled far away.

Bards of Passion and of Mirth,
Ye have left your souls on earth!
Ye have souls in heaven too,
Double-lived in regions new!

1818

THE DOVE

I had a dove and the sweet dove died;
And I have thought it died of grieving:
O, what could it grieve for? Its feet were tied,
With a silken thread of my own hand's weaving;

Sweet little red feet! why should you die?
Why should you leave me, sweet bird! why?
You liv'd alone in the forest-tree,
Why, pretty thing! would you not live with me?
I kiss'd you oft and gave you white peas;
Why not live sweetly, as in the green trees?

1819

If By Dull Rhymes Our English Must Be Chain'd

If by dull rhymes our English must be chain'd,
And, like Andromeda, the Sonnet sweet
Fetter'd, in spite of pained loveliness;
Let us find out, if we must be constrain'd,
Sandals more interwoven and complete
To fit the naked foot of poesy;
Let us inspect the lyre, and weigh the stress
Of every chord, and see what may be gain'd
By ear industrious, and attention meet:
Misers of sound and syllable, no less
Than Midas of his coinage, let us be
Jealous of dead leaves in the bay wreath crown;
So, if we may not let the Muse be free,
She will be bound with garlands of her own.

1819

ON FAME

Fame, like a wayward girl, will still be coy
To those who woo her with too slavish knees,
But makes surrender to some thoughtless boy,
And dotes the more upon a heart at ease;
She is a Gipsey, – will not speak to those
Who have not learnt to be content without her;
A Jilt, whose ear was never whisper'd close,
Who thinks they scandal her who talk about her;
A very Gipsey is she, Nilus-born,
Sister-in-law to jealous Potiphar;
Ye love-sick Bards! repay her scorn for scorn;
Ye Artists lovelorn! madmen that ye are!
Make your best bow to her and bid adieu,
Then, if she likes it, she will follow you.

1819

ON FAME

You cannot eat your cake and have it too. Proverb

How fever'd is the man, who cannot look
Upon his mortal days with temperate blood,
Who vexes all the leaves of his life's book,
And robs his fair name of its maidenhood;
It is as if the rose should pluck herself,
On the ripe plum finger its misty bloom,
As if a Naiad, like a meddling elf,
Should darken her pure grot with muddy gloom:
But the rose leaves herself upon the briar,
For winds to kiss and grateful bees to feed,
And the ripe plum still wears its dim attire,
The undisturbed lake has crystal space;
Why then should man, teasing the world for grace,
Spoil his salvation for a fierce miscreed?

1819

ON MORTALITY

Life is but a Day

TO MY BROTHERS

Small, busy flames play through the fresh laid coals,
And their faint cracklings o'er our silence creep
Like whispers of the household gods that keep
A gentle empire o'er fraternal souls.
And while, for rhymes, I search around the poles,
Your eyes are fix'd, as in poetic sleep,
Upon the lore so voluble and deep,
That aye at fall of night our care condoles.
This is your birth-day Tom, and I rejoice
That thus it passes smoothly, quietly.
Many such eves of gently whisp'ring noise
May we together pass, and calmly try
What are this world's true joys, – ere the great voice,
From its fair face, shall bid our spirits fly.

1816

As from the Darkening Gloom

As from the darkening gloom a silver dove
Upsoars, and darts into the eastern light,
On pinions that nought moves but pure delight,
So fled thy soul into the realms above,
Regions of peace and everlasting love;
Where happy spirits, crown'd with circlets bright
Of starry beam, and gloriously bedight,
Taste the high joy none but the blest can prove.
There thou or joinest the immortal quire
In melodies that even heaven fair
Fill with superior bliss, or, at desire,
Of the omnipotent Father, cleav'st the air
On holy message sent – What pleasure's higher?
Wherefore does any grief our joy impair?

1814

Written in Disgust of Vulgar Superstition

The church bells toll a melancholy round,
Calling the people to some other prayers,
Some other gloominess, more dreadful cares,
More harkening to the sermon's horrid sound.
Surely the mind of man is closely bound
In some blind spell: seeing that each one tears
Himself from fireside joys and Lydian airs,
And converse high of those with glory crowned.
Still, still they toll, and I should feel a damp,
A chill as from a tomb, did I not know
That they are dying like an outburnt lamp, –
That 'tis their sighing, wailing, ere they go
Into oblivion – that fresh flowers will grow,
And many glories of immortal stamp.

1816

To Mrs Reynolds's Cat

Cat! who hast pass'd thy Grand Climacteric,
How many mice and rats hast in thy days
Destroy'd? – How many tit bits stolen? Gaze
With those bright languid segments green, and prick
Those velvet ears – but prithee do not stick
Thy latent talons in me – and upraise
Thy gentle mew – and tell me all thy frays,
Of Fish and Mice, and Rats and tender chick.
Nay, look not down, nor lick thy dainty wrists –
For all thy wheezy Asthma, – and for all
Thy tail's tip is nicked off – and though the fists
Of many a Maid have given thee many a maul,
Still is that fur as soft, as when the lists
In youth thou enter'dst on glass-bottled wall.

1817

After Dark Vapours

After dark vapours have oppressed our plains
For a long dreary season, comes a day
Born of the gentle South, and clears away
From the sick heavens all unseemly stains.
The anxious month, relievèd of its pains,
Takes as a long-lost right the feel of May;
The eyelids with the passing coolness play,
Like rose leaves with the drip of summer rains.
The calmest thoughts come round us – as of leaves
Budding, – fruit ripening in stillness, – autumn suns
Smiling at eve upon the quiet sheaves, –
Sweet Sappho's cheek; – a smiling infant's breath, –
The gradual sand that through an hour-glass runs, –
A woodland rivulet, a Poet's death.

1817

In a Drear-Nighted December

In drear-nighted December
Too happy, happy tree
Thy branches ne'er remember
Their green felicity:
The north cannot undo them
With a sleety whistle through them;
Nor frozen thawings glue them
From budding at the prime

In drear-nighted December
Too happy, happy brook
Thy bubblings ne'er remember
Apollo's summer look;
But with a sweet forgetting
They stay their crystal fretting
Never, never petting
About the frozen time

Ah! Would 'twere so with many
A gentle girl and boy!
But were there ever any

Writhed not at passed joy?
The feel of not to feel it
When there is none to heal it
Nor numbed sense to steel it
Was never said in rhyme.

1817

WHEN I HAVE FEARS THAT I MAY CEASE TO BE

When I have fears that I may cease to be
Before my pen has glean'd my teeming brain,
Before high piled books, in charact'ry,
Hold like rich garners the full-ripen'd grain;
When I behold, upon the night's starr'd face,
Huge cloudy symbols of a high romance,
And feel that I may never live to trace
Their shadows, with the magic hand of chance;
And when I feel, fair creature of an hour!
That I shall never look upon thee more,
Never have relish in the faery power
Of unreflecting love; – then on the shore
Of the wide world I stand alone, and think,
Till Love and Fame to nothingness do sink.

1818

The Human Seasons

Four Seasons fill the measure of the year;
There are four seasons in the mind of man:
He has his lusty Spring, when fancy clear
Takes in all beauty with an easy span:
He has his Summer, when luxuriously
Spring's honied cud of youthful thought he loves
To ruminate, and by such dreaming high
Is nearest unto heaven: quiet coves
His soul has in its Autumn, when his wings
He furleth close; contented so to look
On mists in idleness – to let fair things
Pass by unheeded as a threshold brook.
He has his Winter too of pale misfeature,
Or else he would forego his mortal nature.

1818

HUSH, HUSH! TREAD SOFTLY!

Hush, hush! tread softly! hush, hush my dear!
All the house is asleep, but we know very well
That the jealous, the jealous old bald-pate may hear.
Tho' you've padded his night-cap – O sweet Isabel!
Tho' your feet are more light than a Fairy's feet,
Who dances on bubbles where brooklets meet, –
Hush, hush! soft tiptoe! hush, hush my dear!
For less than a nothing the jealous can hear.

No leaf doth tremble, no ripple is there
On the river, – all's still, and the night's sleepy eye
Closes up, and forgets all its Lethean care,
Charm'd to death by the drone of the humming May-fly;
And the Moon, whether prudish or complaisant,
Hath fled to her bower, well knowing I want
No light in the dusk, no torch in the gloom,
But my Isabel's eyes, and her lips pulp'd with bloom.

Lift the latch! ah gently! ah tenderly – sweet!
We are dead if that latchet gives one little chink!
Well done – now those lips, and a flowery seat –

The old man may sleep, and the planets may wink;
The shut rose shall dream of our loves, and awake
Full blown, and such warmth for the morning's take;
The stock-dove shall hatch her soft brace and shall coo,
While I kiss to the melody, aching all through!

1818

Faery Songs

Shed no tear! oh, shed no tear!
The flower will bloom another year.
Weep no more! oh, weep no more!
Young buds sleep in the root's white core.
Dry your eyes! oh, dry your eyes!
For I was taught in Paradise
To ease my breast of melodies, –
Shed no tear.

Overhead! look overhead!
'Mong the blossoms white and red –
Look up, look up! I flutter now
On this fresh pomegranate bough.
See me! 'tis this silvery bill
Ever cures the good man's ill.
Shed no tear! oh, shed no tear!
The flower will bloom another year.
Adieu, adieu – I fly – adieu!
I vanish in the heaven's blue, –
Adieu, adieu!

Ah! woe is me! poor Silver-wing!
That I must chant thy lady's dirge,
And death to this fair haunt of spring,
Of melody, and streams of flowery verge, –
Poor Silver-wing! ah! woe is me!
That I must see
These blossoms snow upon thy lady's pall!
Go, pretty page! and in her ear
Whisper that the hour is near!
Softly tell her not to fear
Such calm favonian burial!
Go, pretty page! and soothly tell, –
The blossoms hang by a melting spell,
And fall they must, ere a star wink thrice
Upon her closed eyes,
That now in vain are weeping their last tears,
At sweet life leaving, and these arbours green, –
Rich dowry from the Spirit of the Spheres,
Alas! poor Queen!

1818

Why Did I Laugh Tonight?

Why did I laugh tonight? No voice will tell
No god, no demon of severe response
Deigns to reply from heaven or from hell
Then to my human heart I turn at once:
Heart, thou and I are here, sad and alone,
Say, why did I laugh? O mortal pain!
O darkness! darkness! Forever must I moan
To question heaven and hell and heart in vain?
Why did I laugh? I know this being's lease
My fancy to it's utmost blisses spreads
Yet would I on this very midnight cease
And all the world's gaudy ensigns see in shreds
Verse, fame and beauty are intense indeed
But death intenser, death is life's high meed.

1819

La Belle Dame Sans Merci

O what can ail thee, knight-at-arms,
Alone and palely loitering?
The sedge has withered from the lake,
And no birds sing.

O what can ail thee, knight-at-arms,
So haggard and so woe-begone?
The squirrel's granary is full,
And the harvest's done.

I see a lily on thy brow,
With anguish moist and fever-dew,
And on thy cheeks a fading rose
Fast withereth too.

I met a lady in the meads,
Full beautiful – a faery's child,
Her hair was long, her foot was light,
And her eyes were wild.

I made a garland for her head,
And bracelets too, and fragrant zone;

She looked at me as she did love,
And made sweet moan

I set her on my pacing steed,
And nothing else saw all day long,
For sidelong would she bend, and sing
A faery's song.

She found me roots of relish sweet,
And honey wild, and manna-dew,
And sure in language strange she said –
'I love thee true'.

She took me to her Elfin grot,
And there she wept and sighed full sore,
And there I shut her wild wild eyes
With kisses four.

And there she lulled me asleep,
And there I dreamed – Ah! woe betide!
The latest dream I ever dreamt
On the cold hill side.
I saw pale kings and princes too,

Pale warriors, death-pale were they all;
They cried – 'La Belle Dame sans Merci
Thee hath in thrall!'

I saw their starved lips in the gloam,
With horrid warning gaped wide,
And I awoke and found me here,
On the cold hill's side.

And this is why I sojourn here,
Alone and palely loitering,
Though the sedge is withered from the lake,
And no birds sing.

1819

THE DAY IS GONE

The day is gone, and all its sweets are gone!
Sweet voice, sweet lips, soft hand, and softer breast,
Warm breath, light whisper, tender semi-tone,
Bright eyes, accomplish'd shape, and lang'rous waist!
Faded the flower and all its budded charms,
Faded the sight of beauty from my eyes,
Faded the shape of beauty from my arms,
Faded the voice, warmth, whiteness, paradise –
Vanish'd unseasonably at shut of eve,
When the dusk holiday – or holinight
Of fragrant-curtain'd love begins to weave
The woof of darkness thick, for hid delight,
But, as I've read love's missal through to-day,
He'll let me sleep, seeing I fast and pray.

1819

THIS LIVING HAND

This living hand, now warm and capable
Of earnest grasping, would, if it were cold
And in the icy silence of the tomb,
So haunt thy days and chill thy dreaming nights
That thou would wish thine own heart dry of blood
So in my veins red life might stream again,
And thou be conscience-calm'd – see here it is –
I hold it towards you.

1819

INDEX